THE

MVP

Devotional Challenges for Basketball Players

William D. Olin, PhD

Cover photography: Jim Smith
Interior Design: Tami Brumbaugh

CRESCENDO PRESS
Stories that amplify character.

ISBN-13: 978-1945634055
ISBN: 1945634057

Dedication

To the many understanding parents, hardworking players, and patient administrators and assistant coaches who made forty years of coaching enjoyable and fruitful.

But, most of all, this has been possible because of my wife, Barbara. I don't believe there is anything in this world more stressful than being a coach's wife. My career in coaching was only made possible through the spirited, consistent support of Barb. Through all the extensive time requirements of being a college coach; through all the stressful games; through all the ups and downs ... my wife always had my back. She was my rock.

Other Titles Published by Crescendo Press

Kuntent
Paeshunt
Jenurus
Trouble Spot
Monsterella
Made Special
Calm the Quills
Under the Armor
The Vine
Sandstone Cactus
Thanks to Wapiti
Tornadic
Bracelet Brouhaha (The Creekers #1)
Vole Holes (The Creekers #2)
Creek Creature (The Creekers #3)
Crate Fate (The Creekers #4)

Contents

INTRODUCTION 9

ADVERSITY.. 11

BE READY 15

CHOICES 19

COMMITMENT... 23

COMMUNICATION 27

FIRE... 31

FOCUS 34

JUSTICE... 38

KNOW-IT-ALLS 42

MINDSET... 46

MINDSET... 50

NUMBER THREE 53

PEACE.. 57

PERSEVERANCE 61

PT... 65

REFEREES.. 69

RESPONSE 75

ROLES.. 79

SELF-SUFFICIENCY 83

TEAMWORK.. 86

THE ENEMY 90

TOMORROW... 93

WINNING 97

YESTERDAY... 100

1

INTRODUCTION

Through 40 years of coaching—and many more as a player—I have found great similarities and parallels in achieving success on the basketball court and in life as a Christian. The ability to sacrifice personal goals for a greater cause, to treat friend and foe with respect and compassion, to handle stress and disappointment with gentleness and integrity, to follow the rules even though others may be cheating, to persevere through all situations, to believe in yourself and what you are doing ... all of these factors are involved in both basketball and Christian living. I have found basketball to be a great training device for the Christian, a unique opportunity to develop a Christ-like attitude and approach in a variety of situations. I believe basketball not only reveals character but builds it. I invite Christians to play basketball, or at least become involved in some way with the sport.

The following are devotional challenges to Christians and basketball players alike to embrace the qualities that tend to bring success, both on the court and as a servant of our Savior. And the principles and guidelines expressed and exposed in these discussions hold value which extends beyond the realm of basketball, applicable to participants in all team sports and ultimately into the stream of everyday life. Parents and children, employers and employees, leaders and followers will all benefit from the application of the lessons learned through basketball and God's Word.

2

ADVERSITY

"Dear brothers, is your life full of difficulties and temptations? Then be happy, for when the way is rough your patience has a chance to grow. So let it grow, and quit trying to squirm out of your problems. And when your patience is finally in full bloom you will be ready for anything; strong in character, full and complete" (James 1:2-4, TLB).

When peace like a river attendeth my way;
When sorrows like sea billows roll;
Whatever my lot Thou hast taught me to say,
"It is well, it is well with my soul."
--Horatio Spafford and Phillip Bliss

It is difficult to imagine the degree of sorrow felt by Horatio Spafford when he received a telegram informing him that his daughters had drowned in a terrible ocean liner accident. Attempting to work through his despair he wrote the words of this beloved hymn, confirming his faith in God through the darkest of times. Spafford called on his Savior to sustain him through this dark valley in his life, and his faith was rewarded. *"Cast your cares on the Lord and He will sustain you" (Psalm 55:22, NIV).*

Life's tragedies will visit all of us. As Christians we are not immune to difficult situations. Jesus confirmed this in His Sermon on the Mount when He stated, *"He gives His sunshine to both the good and the evil and sends his rain on the just and the unjust too" (Matthew 5:45, TLB).* Scripture also instructs us how to react when adversity enters our lives. We are to accept the fact that bad things *do* happen to good people and trust God in His unlimited power and grace to help us not only survive the tragedy but actually grow stronger through the experience. Such occurrences certainly help strengthen our faith as we are reminded that, no matter how devastating the tragedy, God is able to sustain us even when our strength and resources are spent.

You will note that the recommended response to tragedy was *not* to find fault. The tragedy is multiplied when we become obsessed with finding someone or something to blame. We become consumed by anger and a thirst for vengeance. We need explanations. Or we become immobilized by a prolonged "woe is me" mindset in which we question and doubt God as we attempt to understand how such a thing should happen to us. "What did I ever do to deserve this?" becomes our focus.

Adversity comes in all shapes and sizes to basketball players. Devastating losses in key games, disappointment in your own performance, injuries, bad bounces, bad calls ... all of these are frequent causes of adversity for a typical basketball team. One year our team had its share of adversity in the form of injuries. Our top recruit sustained an injury on the first day of practice that caused her to miss the entire season. Next another key player tore her ACL in the fifth game of the season and was also out for the year. And then our top player off the bench broke her wrist in our first league game. We lost three of our best players. We also lost our depth, were forced to play out of position, had to call up players from the junior varsity...and we had 19 more conference games!

How did our players handle the situation? With character and faith! They did not resort to blaming people, fate, or God for our misfortune. They did not moan and whine about their bad luck or quit trying. They did not lose faith in themselves or in their Savior. The verse, *"I can do all things through Him who gives me strength" (Philippians 4:13, TLB)* took on added significance. The team actually grew stronger through these tough personnel losses. They did not lose faith, even when they suffered lopsided losses in some games. In fact, they never lost two games in a row. They ended up placing third in our 11-team conference and went on to finish second in the nation in the NCCAA National Tournament. They won more games than any women's basketball team in the school's history (at that point). All this was accomplished because they chose the proper response to adversity.

So when you find yourself in a deep valley, don't allow yourself to be consumed with fault-finding, finger-pointing, self-doubt, self-pity, vengeful anger, or a quitter's mentality. Don't lose faith in yourself or others. Trust God to help you triumph over the tragedy. He has promised to help you and He never fails.

He giveth more grace when the burdens grow greater.
He sendeth more strength when the labors increase.
To added affliction He addeth His mercy;
To multiplied trials His multiplied peace.

When we have exhausted our stores of endurance;
When our strength has failed ere the day is half gone;
When we reach the end of our hoarded resources;
Our Father's full giving has only begun!

13

His love has no limit; His grace has no measure;
His power has no boundary known unto man;
For out of His infinite riches in Jesus;
He giveth, and giveth, and giveth again.
-- Annie Johnson Flint

APPLICATION SUGGESTIONS:

1. Learn to embrace adversity. Adversity will visit you, and if you learn to treat it as an opportunity to grow you can not only survive but become stronger because of it. "Life is not all about finding shelter from the storm; it is all about learning how to dance in the rain."

2. Adopt a positive, determined response mode when faced with adversity, so that your teammates, friends, etc., will follow your example and not get caught up in the negative responses so frequently displayed in tough times.

3. Pray for yourself and your teammates that positive growth will take place when trials come your way.

3

BE READY

"The ground of a certain rich man produced a good crop. He thought to himself, 'What shall I do? I have no place to store my crops.' Then he said, 'This is what I'll do. I will tear down my barns and build bigger ones, and there I will store all my grain and all my goods. And I'll say to myself, 'You have plenty of good things laid up for many years. Take life easy. Eat, drink, and be merry.' But God said to him, 'You fool! This very night your life will be demanded from you. Then who will get what you have prepared for yourself?' This is how it will be with anyone who stores up things for himself but is not rich toward God" (Luke 12:16-21, NIV).

There are certainly consequences for not being ready. If you did not prepare adequately for an exam, for instance, you probably failed the test because you were not ready. This is just one example of countless situations in life in which our lack of readiness can result in embarrassment, humiliation, and discouragement. Although quite humbling, in these types of instances we eventually recover. "Life goes on."

But lack of readiness as a Christian has much more dire, permanent consequences. Jesus emphasized the importance of our readiness, both for our death (Luke 12:16-21) and His return

(Matthew 24:42). His urgent message to us as Christians is that we must get ready *now* to meet the Master, because we cannot know when we'll die or when He will come again. The parable of the ten bridesmaids (Matthew 24:1-13) also points out that if you're not ready when the time comes to meet God face to face, you don't get any second chances. So we can't be like the rich man portrayed in Luke 12, who basically became consumed with his own agenda, figuring that he had plenty of time to take care of spiritual matters. Jesus does not want us to make this same mistake. That's why He warns us. All that we do (and accumulate) in life is only momentary. Heaven is forever. So is hell. We need to take care of our spiritual being *now*. God has promised to take care of everything else. Get ready NOW.

Being "ready" in basketball is also extremely important. For a starter this is not nearly as difficult as for a player who rarely sees the court in games. Nevertheless, the true team player is always ready to play, no matter how remote the chances may seem. Several years ago my team was protecting a precarious lead at the end of the game. When a key player fouled out I substituted with an experienced player who was a good ball handler and excellent free throw shooter. But she hadn't played all game and, as it turned out, she wasn't ready for this unexpected turn of events. Consumed by frustration and self-pity because she had not gotten to play up to that point, her un-readiness to play was magnified on the court. We lost the game.

Several seasons later a similar scenario unfolded, but with entirely different results. We were playing in the semi-finals of the NCCAA National Tournament and our slim lead was in jeopardy due to our inability to make free throws and our own foul trouble. Late in the game, with the outcome still in doubt, our fourth player fouled out. I looked down the bench and noticed that Leah, who spends the entire game cheering enthusiastically for her teammates, had suddenly become very quiet. She did the math; she knew she was going in! Three minutes away from qualifying to play for a national championship, I inserted Leah into the fray. Although we missed an incredible total of 18 free throws that game, Leah came through, making 3 of 4, and we won the game. Leah was ready.

There are several reasons for Leah's success. Even though she knew it was doubtful that she would play, she nevertheless sat close to the coaches on the bench, cheering and encouraging her teammates with constant enthusiasm. She stayed "in the game"—she was well aware of all that was going on. She wasn't sitting slumped in her chair at the far end of the bench fretting and stewing about her own lack of playing time. Also, Leah succeeded because she practiced hard. Her attitude wasn't, "If I'm not going to play in the game, why should I work so hard in practice?" But if you watched Leah's intensity level in practice you would have guessed she played all the time.

So the message should be clear. As Christians and as basketball players we must make sure we're always ready. We never know when our name will be called.

"So do not worry, saying 'What shall we eat?' or 'What shall we drink?' or 'What shall we wear?' For the pagans run after all these things, and your heavenly Father knows that you need them. But seek first His kingdom and His righteousness, and all these things will be given to you as well" (Matthew 6:31-33, NIV).

"The Kingdom of Heaven can be illustrated by the story of ten bridesmaids who took their lamps and went to meet the bridegroom. But only five of them were wise enough to fill their lamps with oil, while the other five were foolish and forgot. So, when the bridegroom was delayed, they lay down to rest until midnight, when they were roused by the shout, 'The

17

bridegroom is coming! Come out and welcome him!' All the girls jumped up and trimmed their lamps. Then the five who hadn't any oil begged the others to share with them for their lamps were going out. But the others replied, 'We haven't enough. Go instead to the shops and buy some for yourselves.' But while they were gone, the bridegroom came, and those who were ready went in with him to the marriage feast. And the door was locked. Later, the other five returned. They stood outside, calling, 'Sir, open the door for us!' But he called back, 'Go away! It is too late!' So stay awake and be prepared, for you do not know the date or moment of my return'" (Matthew 25: 1-13, TLB).

APPLICATION SUGGESTIONS:

1. Think back on times in your life when you were well-prepared for something as opposed to being ill-prepared. Were the results of taking the time and effort to prepare thoroughly worth it? Did you gain peace of mind and a sense of accomplishment from "being ready"?

2. When your teammates who don't play much in games give an all-out effort in practice, strive to enthusiastically and sincerely praise their efforts.

3. Make sure that your overriding top priority is always establishing and maintaining the right relationship with God.

4

CHOICES

I saw them tearing a building down;
A group of men in a busy town.
With hefty blow and lusty yell
They swung with zest, and a side wall fell.

I asked the foreman, "Are these men skilled,
The kind you would hire if you wanted to build?"
He laughed and answered, "No indeed;
Unskilled labor is all I need.

Why, they could tear down in a day or two
What it's taken builders years to do."
I asked myself as I walked away,
"Which one of these roles am I trying to play?

Am I a builder with rule and square,
Measuring and constructing with skill and care.
Or am I a wrecker who roams the town,
Content in the business of tearing down?"
        --Anonymous

Basketball teams aren't very democratic by nature. It isn't like the USA, where the leader's power is shared with Congress and the Supreme Court. These checks and balances are designed to prevent anyone (specifically the President) from having absolute power. There is no such arrangement on a typical basketball team. The leader (the coach) dictates what goes on with the team; the players carry out his or her wishes. And, frankly, this system tends to be most effective. Can you imagine the chaos if players could vote to keep or get rid of the coach after every four games? What would happen if a player could insert himself into a game every time he felt like it? What would happen if the players voted on the starting line-up or the plays they would run for each game? There may be some merit to these scenarios but the reality is that the basketball player's role is to simply follow the coach's instructions and play the game. The coach makes the decisions.

This reality must be accepted by the player in order for a team to function properly. In many respects, the player is just a pawn, faithfully carrying out the dictates of the coach. But, besides the obvious importance of the players' efficiency on the court, they also play a key role in the success of the team by their attitude in various situations. As a player you may not have a say as to when you play, what you do in practice, or what plays you run in a game, but you do have a choice on what attitude you display. How you respond to various circumstances, including the decisions your coach makes, is a significant factor in the quality of your team's performance. The decision to not put you in the starting lineup, for example, is made by the coach. You have no voice in that decision. But you *do* have a choice as to how you will respond to not starting. And responses to scenarios such as this have a major impact on your team.

Attitude is important, and it is a choice. Though you do not have control of many of the situations that arise, you *do* have control of your attitude. So what prevails when disappointments or adversity arise? If you are self-centered and possess an inflated ego your response will typically be negative and will impact the team adversely. If you remain upbeat and enthusiastic, however, your attitude will impact your team positively. And your teammates will be affected by your responses. In reference to the above poem, ask yourself this simple question, "Are you a builder or a wrecker?"

This poem also has application to our efforts to live a Christ-like life. Have you ever come across a professing Christian who seems to find fault with everything, who loves to assign blame, who always emphasizes the negative? This is not Christ-like living. Such an attitude is a choice. What we like to call "righteous indignation" is often used as justification to respond with negative judgment to someone who "deserves" to be vilified. But this rationale is unacceptable. James 4:12 states, "...but you—who are you to judge your brother?" Remember when Jesus said, "He who is without sin cast the first stone?" Since we do not deserve God's gift of eternal life through His Son, we have no right to cast judgment on others, even if we think they deserve it. Judgment is God's job, not ours. *Do not let any unwholesome talk come out of your mouths, but only what is helpful in building others up, according to their needs, that it may benefit all who listen" (Ephesians 4:29, NIV).*

Again, are you a builder or a wrecker?

APPLICATION SUGGESTIONS:

1. Look back at your responses (attitude-wise) to past situations which were difficult. Was your choice of attitude a help or hindrance to the efforts of your team to overcome such trials?

2. When difficulties arise, actively take a positive response to the problem. What types of specific attitudinal responses can you make when your team faces adversity?
3. Pray for wisdom to make the proper choices in all situations, choices which will honor God and bring healing to the situation (W.W.J.D.).

5

COMMITMENT

"I know you well. You are neither cold nor hot. I wish you were either one or the other. And because you are merely lukewarm, neither hot nor cold, I am about to spit you out of my mouth" (Revelation 3:15-16, TLB).

The concept of commitment has taken a severe beating in our society in recent years. Marriages, for example, include the sacred vow to stay together "until death us do part," but appalling divorce statistics indicate that the commitment really wasn't there. Too often we tend to put our lives in cruise control, doing enough to comfortably get by, but never enough to excel.

Have you met any "Christians" like that? They were described in Revelation 3:14-19 as the church of Laodicea, a situation Bible scholars believe is common in today's society. Reference is made to people who seem to do all the right things (as long as it's comfortable) but are never totally committed to serving Jesus. Theirs is a God of convenience.

How committed are *you* to serving Jesus? Are you a cruise-control Christian, doing just enough to get by? Is yours a total commitment or a commitment of convenience? Remember the rich young ruler (Matthew 19:16-22)? He was so proud of all the good things he had done, but he went away sorrowful and defeated as Jesus exposed his unwillingness to be *totally* committed to serving Him.

What does it mean to be totally committed to your basketball team? Too many players do not understand the answer to this question. Do you have any players on your team who could be described as having a cruise-control commitment to basketball? They play hard in the games but not in practice; they fudge on making their allotted number of free throws in practice; they run sprints just fast enough to get by. The totally committed basketball player, conversely, plays as hard as he/she can *all* the time. From the routine warm-up drills in practice to the last two minutes of a championship game, the effort of the truly committed player is always 100%.

Not all players have the same talent or potential but all players *are* able to achieve their maximum potential through a total commitment to excellence on the court. Players with cruise-control commitments will never reach their potential, and their team will never achieve its capabilities. Championship teams tend to be filled with players whose commitments to basketball are genuine and total, just as Heaven is filled with people who were 100% committed to serving God. The rewards of a total commitment are awesome, just as the result of cruise-control commitment is unfulfilled potential and ultimate disappointment. Which category describes you?

Commitment involves priorities. Just how committed are you to being the best basketball player you can possibly be; to make the greatest contribution to the success of your team? Giving 100% effort in conditioning, practices, and games reflects a commendable commitment, but if you truly desire to be the *absolute* best you can be, your dedication must go beyond what is required of you. It indicates a greater time commitment to work on your own to improve your skills. Daily shooting practice and dribbling drills are good examples of things you can do on your own time to improve your game. This should include a discipline to continue these personal drills throughout the year, not just during basketball season.

A similar personal discipline should be evident if we are serious about growing in our faith. Regular church attendance, praying before every meal, and putting money in the offering plate are all commendable practices, but in order to truly become all that we could be in Christ we should commit to a daily regimen of personal Bible study and prayer. In this way we will become much more effective as a Christian example and witness, better able to help "Team Jesus" bring the Good News to a lost world.

The quality and quantity of time you spend attempting to better yourself at something reveals your commitment to that endeavor. And whether it's basketball or Christianity, your level of commitment will reveal your priorities. Is your #1 priority your relationship with God? Does it show?

"What is more I consider everything a loss compared to the surpassing greatness of knowing Christ Jesus my Lord, for whose sake I have lost all things. I consider them rubbish, that I may gain Christ" (Philippians 3:8, NIV).

"See to it that you keep on growing in the Lord, becoming strong and vigorous in the truths you were taught" (Colossians 2:7, TLB).

APPLICATION SUGGESTIONS:

1. Commit to improving your game by partnering with a teammate for some extra practice (make 50 free throws per

day; make 25 3's per day; or run a 6-minute mile each day, etc).

2. Commit to improving your relationship with Christ and your life's focus by spending the first 20 to 30 minutes of each day in prayer, devotions, and scripture memorization. Make a prayer list, find a good daily devotional book, memorize a meaningful (to you) passage of scripture each week or two.

3. Make commitments that are very feasible to begin with. You can always make a greater, more time-consuming commitment later on.

6

COMMUNICATION

"Do not let any unwholesome talk come out of your mouth, but only what is helpful in building others up according to their needs, that it may benefit all who listen" (Ephesians 4:29, NIV).

"May the words of my mouth and the meditation of my heart be pleasing in your sight, O Lord, my Rock and my Redeemer" (Psalm 19:14, NIV).

Communication is the lifeblood of society. It would appear that successful means of communication is an absolute essential for the existence of a society in general and relationships in particular. There was never a happier time in my parental life than when my young children finally learned how to talk. They were able to *tell* me what they wanted or needed rather than having me try to guess what the tears and incoherency really meant.

As much as we need communication for creating and maintaining relationships, we can also do great damage with our words. The Scriptures speak of the great harm words can do (Proverbs) and they admonish us to be positive, uplifting, and compassionate in our communication with others. As Christians we can totally undermine our witness with cruel, harsh, judgmental words, spoken in the recipient's presence or behind his back (gossip).

As we continually strive to keep our communication positive and uplifting so that we can enhance instead of undermine the Kingdom of God, we still tend to slip up every now and then. When this happens—when we say things that are hurtful to others—we must take immediate action to rectify the situation. Even if the hurt our words caused was unintentional, we are instructed by Jesus to take immediate action to resolve the issue. *"So if you are standing before the altar in the Temple, offering your sacrifice to God, and suddenly remember that a friend has something against you, leave your sacrifice there beside the altar and go and apologize and be reconciled to him, and then come and offer your sacrifice to God. Come to terms quickly with your enemy ..." (Matthew 5:23-25a, TLB).* In other words, drop what you are doing, go directly to the person you've hurt (or that has hurt you), and make things right. This may be a very difficult, awkward, and humbling experience, but Jesus not only instructs us to do this but promises to help us know what to say in such stressful times. *"Now go; I will help you speak and will teach you what to say" (Exodus 4:12, NIV).*

So what does communication have to do with success on the basketball court? Plenty! Communication on a basketball team can either raise it to new heights as the team becomes an efficiently functioning unit or it can undermine an otherwise talented group, making the record mediocre and the players miserable. If you understand your role as a player and the importance of team unity you will see clearly what type of communication you need to employ. When I first started watching volleyball games I noticed that when a player messed up and lost a point her teammates would immediately join hands with her in a circular "huddle" as if to congratulate her. Initially, I could not understand this. Why congratulate someone for making a bad play? Then it dawned on me that her teammates were not congratulating her but supporting her and encouraging her. This is a perfect illustration of what type of communication should take place among players on a team. When we are uplifting rather than critical with our teammates the team comes together, trusting each other, confident that they are supported "through thick and thin," and free to "give it their best shot" without the paralyzing fear of failure or condemnation from teammates. The team becomes unified and invariably much more successful on the court. In addition, the long season not only becomes tolerable but unbelievably enjoyable, no matter what the final record happens to be.

So let the coach do the (constructive) criticizing—that's his or her job. Your job as a player is to constantly build up your teammates in all situations. They've got to *know* that you've got their back. Refrain from gossip—talking negatively behind someone's back—for this type of communication will tear a team apart. As a Christian and a basketball player the powerful medium of the spoken word can and *must* project a positive, caring, Christ-like attitude as we seek success both on the basketball court and in life.

"Careless words stab like a sword but wise words bring healing" (Proverbs 12:18, TLB).

"If anyone considers himself to be religious but does not hold a tight rein on his tongue, he deceives himself and his religion is worthless" (James 1:26, TLB).

APPLICATION SUGGESTIONS:

1. Make a list (hopefully a short list) of the people in your life you have offended or who have offended you. Has the relationship been restored? If not, take the initiative and go and be reconciled.
2. Do you occasionally or habitually talk negatively behind someone's back? If so, make a conscious effort to refrain from this in the future, and do not participate in such gossip even as a listener.
3. Pray for the Holy Spirit's help in this area. It is a very difficult habit to break.

7

FIRE

"Controlled fire is useful. Uncontrolled fire kills thousands of people and destroys millions of dollars worth of property each year."
--World Book Encyclopedia

As this is being written wildfires are raging out of control in California, Arizona, and Colorado. Thousands of acres have been destroyed and nearly 200 homes have been burned to the ground. Just as all of these families have been devastated by the loss of their home and now must cope with the impact of these fires, so all individuals must face fires of their own in this life. No one is immune. Fires come in the form of financial disasters, relationship meltdowns, serious injury, illness, the death of loved ones and many other events which bring heartache and grief into our lives. Just as these wildfires reduced so many beautiful, expensive homes to a pile of ashes, so the fires in our lives can destroy us. Most of the time when we are victimized by such fires it is through no fault of our own, and this makes them even more difficult to deal with.

Joseph, the favorite of Jacob's twelve sons certainly faced his share of fires in his lifetime: sold into slavery by his own brothers, thrown into prison for crimes he didn't commit,

31

and abandoned by those he helped. The fires in his life were more than enough to destroy him. But they didn't. He actually grew stronger through these difficulties. Joseph realized that fire, when controlled by the proper attitude and response, can be quite beneficial to an individual. Indeed, controlled fire has a myriad of major uses for mankind. Through trust in God, Joseph was able to allow his fires to refine him -- make him a better person. Through his faith he refused to let the fires destroy him. And he ended up as the second most powerful man in all of Egypt, even though he was a foreigner. He came through the fire by trusting in God and landed on his feet.

Fires of all types and levels of severity routinely visit basketball teams. Personnel problems, injuries, losses ... these fires must be dealt with quickly and efficiently. They must be brought under control, because a fire left unchecked will quickly spread, becoming out of control and leaving destruction in its wake. When fire hits your team in the form of a humiliating loss, for instance, it is imperative that you become stronger and increase your faith and resolve through this experience. If left unchecked, such a fire can destroy your self-confidence, team chemistry, and your entire season. Fires will come your way, and they can either refine you or destroy you. It's your choice!

It is also highly recommended that you employ the attributes of fire in your approach to the game. Fire is not just hot, it's *intense*. It's extreme, dominating, and awesomely powerful. Basketball players should play with fire—an intensity level so high it is off the charts. Take charges in practice. Dive after loose balls. When you *always* play with such hustle and determination, the fire in your play will likely spread to your teammates and before you know it your entire team has achieved an intensity level coaches dream about. Then your opponents must deal with the fervor and efficiency of a team on fire.

So make sure, as a Christian and a basketball player, that you don't let the fires that come into your world destroy you. Rather, let them increase your faith and your strength. Then, apply principles of fire to your game plan of serving your Savior and playing on your basketball team. Through the intense, determined nature of your approach, become the spark that ignites others to catch fire.

"Since we are receiving a kingdom that cannot be shaken, let us be thankful, and so worship God with reverence and awe, for our God is a consuming fire" (Hebrews 12:28-9, TLB).

"Dear brothers, is your life full of difficulties and temptations? Then be happy, for when the way is rough your patience has a chance to grow. So let it grow, and quit trying to squirm out of your problems. And when your patience is finally in full bloom you will be ready for anything, strong in character, full and complete" (James 1:2-4, TLB).

APPLICATION SUGGESTIONS:

1. Ask yourself, "Do I play with fire all of the time, or only in certain situations in games?
2. Commit to being fired up every second you are on the court. Your determination and enthusiasm will be noticed and emulated, elevating both your performance and that of your team.
3. Pray for strength to always play with enthusiasm, even when you don't feel like it. Life's situations can really weigh you down and make such fire difficult to maintain at all times, but the Holy Spirit will help you accomplish this difficult task.

8

FOCUS

Turn your eyes upon Jesus
Look full in His wonderful face
And the things of earth will grow strangely dim
In the light of His glory and grace
--Helen Howarth Lemmel

One of the most beneficial and important skills one can ever develop in life is the ability to focus, concentrating totally on whatever is most important at that time. The ability to be 100% focused allows us to perform at maximum efficiency. When we allow anything to distract us, we lose our focus, along with the ability to achieve optimum results, often jeopardizing our chances for success.

Failure as a Christian is normally a result of a lack of focus on Jesus. When you have a decision to make—and we make hundreds of them (great and small) every day—what or who are you focused on when deciding what to do? Is your decision based on what *you* want to do or what your friends might think? It's not necessarily wrong to have our own desires or be concerned with how our actions affect others, but when we make decisions based *only* on these factors we set ourselves up for spiritual failure. When we don't consult Scripture or listen to the Holy Spirit's leading—when we don't ask "What would Jesus do?"—we distance ourselves from God and set ourselves up for spiritual disaster. Our focus is misplaced, and this can be a fatal mistake as we attempt to live a Christ-like life. We have failed to stay focused on the most important aspect of our lives, which is serving God and making choices based on *His* will for us.

Focus is also vitally important in basketball. There are a myriad of potential distractions to a basketball player: a noisy, hostile crowd, parents and friends in attendance, a bad call, a teammate who missed your pass and made you look bad, your own successes and failures in the game, the pressure of the situation. So how can you possibly stay focused with all these things going on? It's really not that difficult. Just subdue your ego enough to let the crowd do the cheering, the officials make the calls, the coaches call the plays, and the other players play their game. This just leaves *yourself* for you to worry about, greatly simplifying the whole situation.

How do you think visiting players in huge arenas can calmly make free throws in pressure situations when the crowd is creating visual mayhem by waving things directly behind the basket and the noise level is absolutely deafening? The best players are not only confident they can make the free throw but are able to tune out all distractions so that they can relax and focus on one particular thing, most likely some part of the rim. If you focus on the right things, in basketball and in life, and refuse to yield to distractions, you will maximize your efficiency in whatever you attempt. True champions never lose their focus, no matter what the situation.

When my wife was pregnant with our second child we enrolled in a childbirth class with several other expectant young couples. These were popular back in the 1970's because they trained fathers to be actively involved in the birthing process.

35

We were to be a coach for our wife during the painful process of labor. I'm not convinced that me telling Barb to *breathe* during contractions did much good to alleviate the pain. Her focal point was far more effective. All expectant mothers in our class were instructed to choose a small but personally meaningful object which would be attached to the ceiling right above her bed during labor. She was to focus on this object, with all its meaning and memories, during the particularly stressful moments in the birthing process. This was an attempt to divert her attention from the pain, and it worked much better than my "coaching" efforts. The application of this principle is also appropriate in our spiritual journey. The best way to resist the temptations of this world and Satan's schemes is to focus on Jesus. It works!

"Set your minds on things above, not on earthly things" (Colossians 3:2, TLB).

"Let us fix our eyes on Jesus, the author and perfecter of our faith" (Hebrews 12:2a, NIV).

APPLICATION SUGGESTIONS:

1. Identify those factors which tend to be on your mind (dominate or interrupt your thoughts) while you are on the basketball court, whether during practice or a game. List them and make a conscious effort to leave all those parts of your life which enter into your thought processes out of the gym so that you can fully concentrate on basketball when you are on the court.
2. In your attempt to live a Christ-like life make sure you are constantly checking in with God when you make decisions both great and small. *"I will instruct you and teach you in*

the way you should go. I will counsel you and watch over you" (Psalm 32:8, NIV). A proper relationship with God and the knowledge of His will is available to you—just as long as He is your focal point.

3. Try to get into the habit of setting certain times or events of your daily routine for "fixing your eyes on Jesus."

9

JUSTICE

"And whatever you say or do let it be as a representative of Christ Jesus" (Colossians 3:17, TLB).

For the longest time the parable Jesus told in Matthew 20 really bothered me. The employer paid the same amount of money to all the workers, whether they had labored all day in the hot sun or whether they just worked one hour in the evening. I didn't understand what the message was. Even though the amount of money paid was indeed a good wage, even for a full day's work, it didn't seem fair. How could it be fair to pay the same wage to people who did a different amount of work? Isn't God supposed to be fair?

When I was finally enlightened to the true message of this parable, it became one of my favorite portions of Scripture, taking my understanding of God and His love to an entirely new level. Indeed, God *isn't* fair! Just as the pay that was given to all the workers that day was more than any of them deserved, even the ones that worked all day, so God's great love for us transcends fair as He offers forgiveness of sins and eternal life for *all* sinners, no matter how sordid our past may be.

And, as Christians, we are expected to take on these same traits in our interaction with society. We are to go beyond justice and exhibit mercy and grace in our everyday lives. Instead of basing actions on the world's eye-for-an-eye mentality, we are instructed to adopt a radical new level of behavior, which is foreign to the thinking of society in general. We are to love our enemies, pray for those who persecute us, return good for evil, and turn the other cheek. It takes a significant attitude adjustment to make the transition from a justice mindset to a grace mindset, but it is not only possible, but also tremendously rewarding. God has already taken care of our present needs and our future security through His Son Jesus. We no longer need to worry about our own ego-driven status here on earth.

As in society, the eye-for-an-eye philosophy is very prominent in the world of basketball. When someone elbows us, aren't we expected to throw an elbow in return? When someone holds your jersey on defense, shouldn't you employ the same tactic? If an opponent is trash-talking, shouldn't you come right back with a clever put-down of your own? NO. Not if, as Christians, we follow God's instructions and live out an attitude of grace.

We are to be different! When someone gets knocked down in the game, regardless of whose team he or she is on or how much they *deserved* to be knocked down, as Christians we help them up. God doesn't want us to pass judgment on whether or not they deserved assistance. It's not our job to judge. We should simply smile and help them up. If our goal is to please God, this is not nearly as difficult as it may seem. Our highest objective should be to represent Christ to everyone we encounter, in all situations. People should be able to see that we are different because we have something the world really needs. We need to understand that if we return elbow for elbow and engage in trash talk with opponents and officials, we are no different than anybody else. Our actions are worldly, not godly.

So, how can a basketball player who is determined to live a Christ-like life, live out his faith on the court? Besides the physical act of helping people up, you can also give verbal affirmations to your opponents when they hustle and/or make a good play. When the whistle blows, hustle to retrieve the ball and give it to the referee. Apologize to your opponent when you unintentionally knock him down. Say, "Good call," to an official, even though the correct call went against you. This action would probably delay the game a bit—the startled referee will need a little extra time to recover from the shock.

It is customary to give your teammate physical acknowledgement when he makes, or even misses, a free throw. I was recently watching a junior high game when a player made a free throw and an *opposing* player gave him a congratulatory hand slap! Now that's different. It's Christ-like. Such unusual acts of sportsmanship must be sincere and genuine to be truly appreciated. There is no room for sarcasm here. It's all about respect.

I understand that there would be many Christian coaches and players who might be very skeptical of such a radical approach. I am convinced, however, that you can be a champion of grace on the court and still be intense and competitive. It really all comes down to who you are playing for. If you're playing for yourself and your own ego needs or to impress someone else, your actions on the court will probably be no different than anybody else's. But if, as a Christian, you are truly playing for God you will be able to exhibit grace on the court, with peace in your heart and a smile on your face. In life and on the basketball court, do people see Christ in you?

"Live your life in such a way that people who know you but don't know God will come to know God because they know you."
- Anonymous

40

APPLICATION SUGGESTIONS:

1. Look back on your own experiences on the basketball court. How did you react when someone cheated, bad-mouthed you, or displayed poor sportsmanship towards you? Did you react appropriately or should you have given a different response?
2. Make a list of all the ways you could be Christ-like on the court, rather than giving conventional responses to various situations. How can you be different and thereby make a difference for Christ? *"Do not conform any longer to the patterns of this world but be transformed by the renewing of your mind..." (Romans 12:2, NIV).*

10

KNOW-IT-ALLS

"Only fools refuse to be taught" (Proverbs 1:7b, TLB).

"It's what you learn after you know it all that counts."
--John Wooden

Did you ever run into someone who thought they had all the answers? We tend to label these types of people know-it-alls because they come across as people who can't be told anything—they already have the answer. To the know-it-all there are always two ways of looking at things; their way and the wrong way.

The Holy Scriptures are full of tragic illustrations of know-it-alls who met their demise. King Saul is one example. He decided not to follow all of God's instructions, choosing instead to do things his way in certain instances. This led to trouble for both Saul and the people of his kingdom. He was never the same. The Pharisees whom Jesus denounced so vehemently are a graphic example of people who became so enthralled with their own knowledge that their minds became closed and their hearts became hardened. In their own self-important mindsets they refused to consider anything as true that would go against their own ideas and threaten their exalted status.

When we stop studying and consulting the Scriptures and when we stop seeking the guidance of the Holy Spirit we have, in essence, become spiritual know-it-alls. We have come to believe that our knowledge is more than sufficient to meet the challenges and decisions that come our way. While it is admirable to have gained knowledge and be confident in our abilities to parlay that knowledge into wise decisions, it is folly to think that there is no more wisdom to be gained from One who knows more than we do. Do you really think you know more than God? Will you close out any possibility of learning from your Creator? Do you really think you know that much? The reality is this: not only does God know more than us but so does Satan! If we close out God we will be destroyed by Satan, no matter how wise we think we are. *"For the wisdom of this world is foolishness in God's sight"* (I Corinthians 3:19, NIV).

A know-it-all basketball player can devastate a team. Just as the results are disastrous when a Christian leaves God out of the picture, so it will lead to the demise of a basketball team if they resist or ignore their coach. Just as God knows more than His created beings, coaches know more about the game of basketball than their players. Through teaching, correction, and exhortation it is the coach's responsibility to help his players and his team be as efficient as possible on the court. These efforts are undermined, however, when players won't listen to their coach. Even more problems occur when players begin disagreeing with their coach through verbal confrontation and their actions on the court. Such situations lead to chaos, confusion, and the ultimate demise of the team.

Do you really believe you know as much as your coach, or do you truly think that your basketball skills and knowledge are so good that there's nothing your coach can really teach you—that there's no room for improvement? Think again! Unlike God, your coach isn't perfect and does make occasional mistakes, but he is still able to help you as a player and your team as a unit increase in skill and efficiency. Your job is to simply listen and trust that the coach knows what he is talking about. If the coach decides to play a zone defense, for instance, that may indeed be the proper strategy for the situation, but the defense will still be ineffective unless the players buy in to the zone strategy. If they question the coach's decision they will have a difficult time making the zone work properly.

We don't always understand God and His dealings with us, and we sometimes don't understand our basketball coach's decisions. But we must remember our role. To be an effective Christian we need to trust God's wisdom rather than our own. Players on an efficient basketball team need to listen to their coach and carry out his instructions with confidence, commitment, and 100% effort. Don't run the risk of being labeled a know-it-all.

"The wise man is glad to be instructed, but a self-sufficient fool falls flat on his face" (Proverbs 10:8, TLB).

"To learn you must want to be taught. To refuse reproof is stupid" (Proverbs 12:1, TLB).

"A fool thinks he needs no advice, but a wise man listens to others" (Proverbs 12:18, TLB).

APPLICATION SUGGESTIONS;

1. Ask yourself: Are you so close-minded in certain situations that you are not able to accept and/or process different ideas or strategies? If so, commit to keeping an open mind so that

you can be receptive to new and possibly better ways to think and do various things.
2. Forge in yourself a mindset that is excited to hear different ideas, admitting to yourself that you really don't know everything.
3. Be careful, as you try to become more broad-minded, that the principles outlined in God's Holy Word should never be compromised.

11

MINDSET
(PART ONE)

If you think you are beaten, you are. If you think you don't dare, you don't.
If you'd like to win but think you can't, it's almost a cinch you won't.

If you think you might lose, you've lost. For out in this world you'll find
That success begins in a fellow's will. It's all in the state of mind.

If you think you're outclassed, you are. You've got to think high to rise.
You've got to be sure of yourself before you can ever win the prize.

Life's battles aren't always won by the faster or stronger man,
For sooner or later the one who wins is the one who <u>thinks</u> he can.

   --Anonymous

Former star baseball player Yogi Berra once remarked that hitting is "90% mental and the other half physical." Yogi's math is certainly suspect but he makes a good point. One's mental approach to any athletic endeavor, whether it is hitting a baseball, shooting a free throw, throwing a pass, or making a putt, is a vital component to the result of the performance. Indeed, the mindset of the performer as he or she attempts a skill or enters a contest is often the deciding factor between victory and defeat, success and failure.

As a college women's basketball coach I became keenly aware of the importance of our mental approach to each game. Sure, the physical preparation was predominant and ongoing, but the attitude with which we entered the game was also vital to our success. If we were to maximize our potential in a given contest we could not allow ourselves to become distracted by our opinion of our opponent. If they were a team we had previously beaten and had a losing record, it would be easy to be overconfident. Conversely, if they were a very good team it would be just as easy to enter the game with fear and doubt. Either way, such mindsets would deter us from playing up to our capabilities.

Every season I would pick one or two pre-season (non-league) games to test a theory. I would give absolutely no information to our team regarding our opponent—we would be entering the contest blind. This caused us to totally rely on our own training and preparation regarding the basic skills and procedures we adhere to as a team, making the necessary adjustments as the game wore on. We were totally focused on what we do as team, not distracted by any pre-conceived merits of our opponent. We trusted our own preparation to be able to compete successfully with any team, no matter what their past performances may have been. It really worked quite well. The results were positive.

This concept is certainly important as we attempt to live Christ-like lives. We are commissioned to bring the message of the Gospel to a needy world by our words, deeds, and attitudes. We must know our spiritual playbook, the Bible, to be effective in this endeavor, just as a basketball team must know its plays and fundamental strategies. But if the Christian, when facing the opportunities which arise each day, comes across as overconfident (a "holier than thou" attitude) or fearful (afraid to say or do the wrong thing or be vilified) he/she will not be an effective witness. The problem? TRUST! Just as a basketball team must trust its coach, so the Christian must trust his/her Savior and playbook (the Bible) in order to boldly and humbly be Christ-like in all situations. Christians who come across as arrogant, fearful, or anxious are not displaying the proper mindset. Why worry? God has our back!

"You are to lead clean, innocent lives as children of God in a dark world full of people who are stubborn and crooked. Shine out among them like beacon lights, holding out to them the Word of life" (Philippians 2:15-16, TLB).

"Will all your worries add a single moment to your life?" (Matthew 6:27, TLB).

"Cast all your anxieties on Him, for He cares for you" (1 Peter 5:7, NIV).

"Make up your mind not to worry beforehand how you will defend yourself. I will give you words and wisdom that none of your adversaries can resist or contradict" (Luke 21:15, TLB).

"Be strong and courageous. Do not be terrified. Do not be discouraged. For the Lord your God will be with you wherever you go," (Joshua 1:9, NIV).

APPLICATION SUGGESTIONS:

1. Look back at certain games you lost when you should have won. Did overconfidence and not taking your opponent seriously play a role in this unlikely setback? If so, make the commitment to enter every contest, no matter how theoretically weak the other team is, with an attitude of genuine respect for your opponent.

2. Have you ever entered games with very talented opponents with fear? Did this result in a lack of confidence and an inevitable defeat? If so, commit to eliminating the debilitating attitude of fear that can destroy any chance of beating a quality opponent.

3. Trust God in all situations (Proverbs 3:5). Memorize some key scriptures that will help you do this and experience the joy of eliminating fear, worry, and anxiety from your mindset as you enter a potential stressful and challenging situation.

4. Adopt a "Respect everyone and fear no one" mindset as you enter every game.

12

MINDSET
(PART TWO)

If you think you are beaten, you are. If you think you don't dare, you don't.
If you'd like to win but think you can't, it's almost a cinch you won't.

If you think you might lose, you've lost. For out in this world you'll find
That success begins in a fellow's will. It's all in the state of mind.

If you think you're outclassed, you are. You've got to think high to rise.
You've got to be sure of yourself before you can ever win the prize.

Life's battles aren't always won by the faster or stronger man,
For sooner or later the one who wins is the one who <u>thinks</u> he can.
--Anonymous

The greatest compilation of athletes on the planet meets every four years in the Olympic Games to see who is the best in a variety of athletic endeavors. The eyes of the world are glued to this three-week extravaganza more than on any other international event. Winners become wealthy, famous, and even legendary. The pressure is enormous!

In the 1976 Summer Olympiad in Montreal, Canada, there were many outstanding, record-setting performances, but the most amazing exhibition of athletic proficiency came from a diminutive 14-year-old Romanian gymnast named Nadia Comaneci. Nadia shocked the gymnastics world by scoring the first perfect "10" in Olympic history when she performed a flawless routine on the uneven parallel bars. She went on to score no less than seven perfect tens in various events throughout the competition. Her perfection caused the international gymnastics community to change their scoring system. How could a 14-year-old travel halfway around the world and perform so flawlessly in the largest, most visible, pressurized venue in the world? When asked this question Nadia simply stated that she was confident that she could "stick" each routine because she did it all the time in practice.

PRACTICE! She *would* have to say that! Not superior talent? Not excellent coaching? No, just one simple word— practice. In the above poem I would call your attention to the third verse, second line: "You've got to be sure of yourself before you can ever win the prize." And there is only one way to be sure of yourself, to be totally confident no matter what the pressure or the situation. Nadia *practiced* to the point that she knew she could perform her routines successfully in any situation or circumstance.

Simply stated, if you commit to something and truly desire to become as proficient as your potential would allow, you must discipline yourself to practice. Repetitive perseverance, working through disappointments, never settling for mediocre effort or performance—these are all qualities of the type of practice that will enable you to eventually become the best you can be at whatever you are trying to achieve.

The applications to basketball teams are obvious, but what does practice have to do with Christianity? Everything! Jesus said in his famous Sermon on the Mount that we

51

(Christians) are to be perfect just as our Father in heaven is perfect (Matthew 5:48). How do we accomplish this perfection? Take the same approach Nadia took. Just as she had to learn the different techniques and procedures encompassed in her various routines, so the Christian first needs to learn what is expected of him/her. This knowledge, of course, is found in our spiritual playbook, the Bible. Once we know what we ought to do we need to practice these attitudes and actions which make up the Christ-like lifestyle. Walk the talk. Practice what you preach. Commitment to living for Jesus is a daily challenge and opportunity. If this is important to you, learning the expectations (memorizing scripture) and carrying out these precepts in the various situations of life (loving your enemies, being compassionate and forgiving) should be a constant focus for you.

Remember that we will all slip up occasionally and act or react in a way that is not Christ-like, but we simply need to learn from our mistakes and get better. Nadia did not *always* achieve perfection. But that was her goal and she worked hard through the disappointments to be successful. Just as the apostle Paul made some poor choices along the way, so his desire was to "*strain* to reach the end of the race and receive the prize for which God is calling us up to heaven" (Philippians 3:14, TLB). So keep straining. God will help you through the rough times, and great will be your reward in heaven.

APPLICATION SUGGESTIONS:

1. Discipline yourself to put just as much effort into practice as you do in games, knowing that the harder you practice, the better you will do in the game.
2. Rather than thinking of practice as a necessary evil, commit to the mindset that treats practice as a great opportunity to get better at something you really enjoy.
3. Practice Christianity by being consistent and dedicated (on a daily basis) to connecting with God and growing in His Word.

13

NUMBER THREE

"Have it your way." "You deserve a break today." "Looking out for #1." "Do your own thing." Our country's culture has had a fascination with the exaltation of self for the past 50 years. We are an unbelievably self-centered society. Our priorities in life seem to not only begin with, but also be dominantly consumed by, our quest to fulfill our own needs and desires. This "It's all about me" mentality pervades every aspect of our society, including the world of sports. When a football player makes a key tackle or scores a touchdown, does he react with a celebration of "Look how great I am" antics or does he seek out the teammates that aided his effort and give them some credit?

Ryan was a standout prep basketball player, highly recruited by several colleges. He finally chose to play at a small midwestern university and was an immediate key contributor to the success of his team. He was a returning starter as he approached his senior year, but his coach was faced with a dilemma: he had six players who were very talented and deserved to be starters. Ryan, of course was one of these. His coach, who was very fond of Ryan, nevertheless put the welfare of the team ahead of the individual (as all good coaches do) and came to the difficult decision to not start Ryan. After being a starter and a senior, Ryan could have easily and understandably been upset and resentful of this, but Ryan was one who put the team ahead of himself. As a result, Ryan played a key role coming off the bench that year, showing his value and versatility as he played several positions as the circumstances mandated. His team won the national championship, the first in his school's history. This happy ending was all made possible because Ryan placed the welfare of the team ahead of his own goals. He basically went against society's norm of placing self above all other priorities.

John Wooden, probably the greatest basketball coach of all time, recalled an interesting story involving one of his star players, Bill Walton, as UCLA embarked on the quest for yet another national title. Walton, easily the best college player in the nation at that time, came into Coach Wooden's office after a 10-day layoff sporting a beard. UCLA had a rule forbidding facial hair on their players. Coach Wooden recalled the ensuing conversation with Walton.

"Bill, have you forgotten something?"

"Coach, if you mean the beard, I think I should be allowed to wear it. It's my right."

"Do you believe that strongly?"

Walton answered, "Yes, I do, coach. Very much."

Coach Wooden looked at him and said politely, "Bill, I have a great respect for individuals who stand up for those things in which they believe. I really do. And the team is going to miss you."

Bill went to the locker room and shaved the beard off before practice began.

Coach Wooden later said, "There were no hard feelings. I wasn't angry and he wasn't mad. He understood the choice was between his own desires and the good of the team. And Bill was a team player."

Both of these examples illustrate the way we are supposed to prioritize. A team can only reach its full potential when the players and the coach put the interests of the team above their own interests, no matter how it affects their egos. The Christian life carries with it a similar reality. The Scriptures plainly point out that our highest priority should be God, not ourselves. Jesus plainly states that to love God is the most important commandment, and that to love your neighbor as yourself is number two. And when we plug in Romans 12:10b ("...honor one another *above* yourselves") the tie between ourselves and others is broken. The result? God is #1, others are #2, and we are #3! That goes against the grain of the typical mindset in our current culture, but it is clearly the way God wants us to prioritize out lives. For Ryan all along, God as #1, others (team) as #2, and me (Ryan) as #3 was a reality. And these priorities were lived out for him as a college basketball player. True peace, happiness, and joy will come to us if we, too, embrace this philosophy and approach to life. Everybody seems so concerned about striving to be #1, but if we can truly say "I'm #3" we can know that whatever happens, we win in the end.

"Love the Lord your God with all your heart, with all your soul, with all your mind, and with all your strength" (Mark 12:30, NIV).

"Be devoted to one another in brotherly love. Honor one another above yourselves" (Romans 12:10, NIV).

APPLICATION SUGGESTIONS:

1. Goals are very important and useful. Be sure that your most important goals are team-oriented rather than me-oriented.

2. Realize that your relationships, both in basketball and in life, will be much more productive and genuine if you take the "I'm #3" attitude rather than always placing your wants and desires as the top priority.
3. Ask God to show you how your attitude could become less selfish and more about God and others.

14

PEACE

"Lord, make me an instrument of Thy peace. Where there is hatred let me so love; where there is injury, pardon; where there is doubt, faith; where there is despair, hope; where there is darkness, light; where there is sadness, joy. O, Divine Master, grant that I may not so much seek to be consoled as to console; to be understood as to understand; to be loved as to love. For it is in giving that we receive. It is in pardoning that we are pardoned. It is in dying that we are born to eternal life."
--Prayer of Saint Francis of Assisi

"Let the peace of heart which comes from Christ be always present in your hearts and lives, for this is your privilege and responsibility as members of His body" (Colossians 3:15, TLB).

Peace is one of the most sought-after, yet unfulfilled, goals of society. Although man places a very lofty value on peace, his own sinful nature usually takes precedence, resulting in a state of constant strife and warfare between families, communities, and nations. It is not surprising, then, that when Jesus came preaching a gospel of peace, compassion, and forgiveness they killed Him. So powerful was His message that He lived it out, even through His death on the cross. The Son of God could have just snapped his fingers and exterminated all of His opposition, but His message of peace and His mission would have been unfulfilled had He done so. As the song goes, "He could have called ten thousand angels but He died alone for you and me."

As Christians we are instructed to be peacemakers in a society that is mostly self-centered, aggressive, judgmental, and confrontational. This is not an easy task, but it is our Christian responsibility. Peacemaking goes against the grain of current societal values, but God will help us follow his Son's example and send a message of peace to a violent world of self-centered inhabitants. He has also promised to give us opportunities to show the peace of heart, which has been given to us as Christians, to a needy world. In reality, our opportunities to be peacemakers abound. Every relationship we have, every encounter with another human being, gives us a chance to display an attitude of grace, patience, humility, and forgiveness. Are you willing to turn the other cheek? Jesus was. He paid the ultimate price, and He did it just for you and me. So the least we can do is follow His example by subduing our ego and our self-centered, sinful nature and becoming true peacemakers.

It becomes quite clear how important peacemakers are on a basketball team. Team chemistry—a special togetherness—is a highly valued characteristic of a championship unit. The attitude of respect, understanding, patience, and forgiveness of the peacemaker is essential in forming a unit which will be able to achieve this chemistry to stay together through all situations.

I once had a player come to my office with a very concerned look on her face. She confided that she just did not like one of her teammates. It was basically just a personality thing, but she was very troubled about her attitude towards this

58

individual. We all know people who really bug us, who seem to be so different in so many ways, especially in the area of personality. I admired this player for being so concerned with the team unity issue here and the need to be together as a unit.

If you are ever faced with a similar situation, ask God to help you to take a different approach to your relationship by *accepting* the personality differences and dwelling on whatever good qualities you can find in this person. The patience, understanding, and positive spirit you display to this individual as a peacemaker will make a great difference and, as the peacemaker you will *receive* a peace in this relationship that you never thought possible. If the relationship is so strained that a face-to-face meeting is needed, Jesus instructs us to, without hesitation, meet with this individual and, with the attitude and grace of a peacemaker, mend whatever is broken in the relationship (Matthew 5:23-26).

Chemistry is an essential ingredient for successful teams—teams that are able to achieve their full potential. And this chemistry can only be achieved through players who live out the peacemaker qualities described and demonstrated by the ultimate proponent and giver of peace, Jesus Christ. Are you a peacemaker on your team?

"The best teams have chemistry. They communicate with each other and they sacrifice personal glory for a common goal."
 --Dave DeBusschere

"Blessed are the peacemakers ..." (Matthew 5:9, NIV).

APPLICATION SUGGESTIONS:

1. Analyze your team's chemistry. How are you affecting it?

2. List some of the attitudes and actions which can adversely affect team chemistry.

3. Then take a good inward look. What areas can you change in your behavior that would help improve team chemistry?

4. Is there an individual on the team that you need to make peace with? If so, take the first step to remedy the situation, carrying with you the same attitude Christ would have.

15

PERSEVERANCE

"The night before Herod was to bring him to trial, Peter was sleeping between two soldiers, bound with two chains, and sentries stood guard at the entrance" (Acts 12:6-7, NIV).

Things didn't look good for Peter. He was in prison, bound with chains and so thoroughly guarded that escape was humanly impossible. His trial was set for the next morning but everyone knew it was a mere formality. Herod had recently arrested and executed the apostle James, much to the delight of the Jews. Peter would be next. But Peter's friends did not give up hope. They chose not to spend their time planning an elaborate, spectacular jail-break. They knew this would be impossible. Instead, they prayed with fervor to the One they knew was their only real hope if Peter were to be spared. And their prayers were answered. *"And pray in the spirit on all occasions with all kinds of prayers and requests. With this in mind, be alert, and always keep on praying for all the saints" (Ephesians 6:18, NIV).*

In his rematch with heavyweight champion Apollo Creed in *Rocky II*, Rocky Balboa was once again in constant trouble from the outset of the fight. Creed, obviously the superior boxer, had administered a severe beating to the challenger by the end of the second round. But Rocky's greatest asset was his heart. He should have been knocked out, but he didn't quit. He had every *right* to quit -- his skills were noticeably inferior and he was getting pummeled. He was already guaranteed a healthy paycheck, win or lose, and he was in grave danger of doing permanent damage to his eye. But he got up again and again and again. The odds didn't matter. His character wouldn't allow him to quit. He still believed he could win. He persevered, and eventually won the fight, allowing all of us an opportunity to look forward to *Rocky III*.

Both of the above examples illustrate the power and reward of perseverance—pressing ahead to achieve a goal even though the odds are overwhelmingly against us. As a teacher of physical education several years ago I was shocked and saddened that my junior high students, even though they loved to play basketball, would choose not to play at all if they thought they were going to lose. Christianity would no longer *exist* if all Christians took that attitude. Paul, who had more than his share of traumatic setbacks, nevertheless kept straining to reach the goal. We are to follow his example. ***"I strain to reach the end of the race and receive the prize for which God has called us up to heaven, because of what Christ Jesus did for us" (Philippians 3:14, TLB).***

Our last regular season game was against our arch-rival. They were nationally ranked and had already beaten us earlier in convincing fashion. So when we fell behind by 16 points at halftime there didn't appear to be much hope. But we didn't quit, and we went on to outscore our opponent, 52-27, in the second half and achieve a very improbable victory. How did this happen? First of all, we didn't panic. We made a couple of minor strategic adjustments at halftime, but basically stuck with what had worked for us all year. We didn't take outrageous gambles on defense or shoot a barrage of three-pointers, hoping to bank some in and get back into the game. Secondly, we didn't lose our confidence. Just as Peter's friends continued to pray and believe that God could deliver Peter, each player on our team continued to believe in their ability and that of their teammates. Thirdly, we played with heart. Just as Rocky's great heart pulled him through, our team played with such heart and determination that victory still remained feasible in the face of great odds.

Remember, an attitude of perseverance—of never giving up—will not always result in victory by the world's standards. Peter was eventually crucified. Rocky was battered by "Mr. T" in *Rocky III*. And one week after our stirring comeback victory we were victimized by another team's come-from-behind triumph against us. But the most important thing is that we keep playing hard, believing in ourselves and our teammates. So don't panic. Don't quit. Keep the faith. People who persevere are always rewarded, in one way or another.

"Size is not the measure of a man's worth, unless you're talking about the size of his heart."
--Wilt Chamberlain

APPLICATION SUGGESTIONS:

1. Were you ever in a situation when you prematurely gave up? Don't feel bad; we've all been there. But the important thing is to realize that quitting early is not wise, and the determination to keep trying (even when the odds are against you) always gives you a chance to pull out an improbable victory and at least give you the satisfaction of knowing that you gave it your best shot. "You're only a loser if you quit trying." - Mike Ditka

2. When you feel like quitting—and the situation seems hopeless—remember that nothing is impossible with God (Luke 1:37).

3. So adopt a persevere to the end approach to life's challenges, knowing that you will not only benefit from such a mindset but you will positively affect others in your sphere of influence.

16

PT

"God does not promise us freedom from our circumstances; He promises us freedom within our circumstances."
--Earl Lee

Dick Vitale, the colorful ambassador of college basketball, has added a military touch to the sport by popularizing abbreviations and initials for some of the more standard basketball terms. "Can he shoot the 'J' (jumpshot)?" "His 'PT' (playing time) has been down lately." We may not care at all if he can shoot the J but all of us (especially players and parents) have a keen interest in PT.

When Americans Martin and Gracia Burnham, missionaries to the Philippines, were abducted by terrorists, Christians all over the world earnestly prayed for their safe release throughout their year in captivity. But when they were finally freed Martin lost his life while Gracia, although injured, survived. Gracia would recover, be reunited with her family, and go on in service for her Lord. Her husband, however, had run out of PT. For Martin the game was over. In our grief and dismay we tend to ask God how He could let one of His faithful servants meet such an untimely, premature demise. We must remember, however, that to question God is not the proper response. God's wisdom is so great that we cannot ever hope to understand, so we shouldn't waste our time asking, "Why?" Just trust God. Keep your faith. God knows what is best and He never fails those who trust Him. *"For the wisdom of this world is foolishness in God's sight" (1 Corinthians 3:19, NIV).*

Gracia Burnham's faith never wavered, even when dealing with her husband's death. Her faith intact, she spoke of the Burnham homecoming when she returned to the States. She commented that they both had come home, Gracia to her family in Kansas and Martin to his Savior in heaven. Gracia still has more PT. She will probably continue to enthusiastically serve the Lord in whatever capacity He chooses for her rather than spend her time questioning and doubting God. *"And we know that in all things God works for the good of those who love Him, who have been called according to His purpose" (Romans 8:28, NIV).*

PT is a major concern for any basketball player ... and it *should* be. If you are content to sit on the bench game after game, why are you even on the team? It is my desire, as coach, to have *all* my players diligently and with determination seek more playing time. And players should take note of a factor coaches are already well aware of: that virtually every player on the team, including some of the starters, wants more playing time. Most feel they *deserve* more playing time.

This provides one of the coach's greatest challenges—dealing with a team full of players who are unhappy with their PT. In my first year in college I was on the freshman team. I was a guard on a team full of guards and, although I was confident I was as skilled as any of them, I ended up what amounted to fourth string in the scheme of things on that team. When you're fourth string, a whole lot of players have to foul out before you see the court. Needless to say, I was not thrilled with my (lack of) PT. I had several choices at that point. I could quit. I could stay on but just go through the motions. (What good would it do to play hard in practice when there was little chance of getting in the game?) I could be critical of the coach and display a bad attitude. Or I could react to the situation by continuing to work hard and stay positive. I chose the latter, not because I was some kind of special person but because I simply loved the game too much and I was not brought up to be a complainer or a quitter. It was the right choice.

The season often provided a great challenge to me and my team because I had twelve talented players who could legitimately claim their rights to considerable PT. And we all know that twelve players getting their desired PT is impossible. So what should these players do? They should work hard to accept their coach's decision with a positive attitude and work even harder to change his mind through effort and improvement in practice. Spend your time doing, not questioning. And be ready! You never know when the coach might call your name, making that treasured PT a reality.

APPLICATION SUGGESTIONS:

1. Are you unsure of why you are not playing more in the games? The proper approach to this common situation is to meet with your coach, one on one, to discuss the situation. He/she will let you know the reasoning regarding your PT and will give you suggestions as to the specific skills you should work on to improve your chances of earning more playing time.
2. If your PT is not what you had hoped for, don't make the mistake of interpreting this as a sign that you are no good. Remember that if your PT is down, your skill level can still be very good but your teammates' skill level may be even better. Don't get down on yourself.

3. Your earthly PT is but a heartbeat compared to eternity, so treasure every moment.

17

REFEREES

"There is a saying, 'Love your friends and hate your enemies.'
But I say: Love your enemies! Pray for those who persecute
you! In that way you will be acting as true sons of your Father
in heaven" (Matthew 5:44-45, TLB).

"I think that I shall never see a satisfactory referee."
    --Larry Neuman

In His "Sermon on the Mount" Jesus squashes the eye-for-an-eye mentality which was so popular and prevalent, both in Jesus' day and in today's society. Loving our enemy goes totally against the grain of popular modern thought, yet that is what we as Christians are instructed to do. Jesus not only told us how to act but He also lived it out during His brief time on earth. As the song goes, "He could have called ten thousand angels but He died alone for you and me." So we're supposed to treat all people, even those with whom we have a major problem, with kindness, patience, understanding, gentleness, compassion, and forgiveness.

This can be quite a challenge at times, especially when we enter the gym and encounter those dreaded people who wear black and white striped shirts and have whistles around their neck. For those of us who love both Jesus and basketball, the referee can pose a significant problem and challenge to our beliefs. Our ability to deal with referees and their imperfections in a Christ-like manner is not only a major challenge, but also a great opportunity for Christian growth and witness. It is very fashionable and acceptable in our society to criticize officials in a way that is not Christ-like. It is so prevalent that it appears that even Christians have claimed the right to join in the barrage of verbal abuse directed at referees. Where did we ever get the idea that Jesus' teachings and instructions to us pertained to everyone except referees? Whether a player, coach, or spectator, our attitude towards referees should be vastly different from the accepted norm.

This may seem very difficult, but when we look more closely at the referee—his persona, his knowledge, his motivation, his challenges—we should be able to be more compassionate to these embattled officials. We must realize that the referee is not the enemy. He is not out to get you. You need to understand why most people become referees: it's not because they want to make your team lose; it's not because they enjoy being yelled at; it's not because they're on a power trip; it's certainly not because of the money. People referee mostly because they love the game and want to make it better for the players. We must also take into account the enormity of their task. Even though they know the rules better and are the only unbiased people in the building, referees are faced with one of the most difficult tasks invented by man. To instantly make the correct call (or no call) in such a fast-paced, contact-laden contest, and to do it with consistent efficiency and unswerving accuracy, is an impossible task for two or three people. We must come to grips with this reality.

Referees are human and they make mistakes, just like all of us do. But they deserve the understanding and respect Jesus prescribed to us as Christians just as much as any other element in society. So be encouraging and supportive of referees. They're doing their best. Cut them some slack and don't for a second think you could do a better job.

My personal struggle with this issue, both as a player and as a coach has been ongoing now for 50 years. Although it has been difficult I feel I have made significant progress. I wrote the following poem in the early 1970's in an attempt to come to grips with my attitude towards referees. It was, and still is, a very important issue for me, because my goal of representing Christ in all I do as a Christian is simply not compatible with yelling at referees. If I am rude, obnoxious, or unkind to referees while claiming to be a Christian, I consider myself nothing more than a hypocrite, and my witness to others becomes worthless. Maybe this poem can help you like it did me.

ODE TO A REFEREE

Basketball is one fast sport;
players sprinting up the court.
Some are jumping, some are running;
some are walking, some are gunning.

To bring some order to the play
are many rules we must obey;
From steps to blocking to "3 in the key"
to a charge on number 53.

Ten men all moving frantically
and breaking rules quite frequently.
And who is charged to keep the peace?
Two very human referees!

71

He calls the rules right to the letter
but someone always sees it better.
And someone always must inject,
"Hey ref, go get your eyesight checked.

He charged me like a guided missile
but you didn't even blow the whistle.
He obviously touched my arm
but you just say, "No foul, no harm."

I can't believe you called that foul.
He didn't even yell or howl.
He only bled a little bit!
Good gracious, ref, you're sure unfit.

A technical on me? How punk!
I'd sure like to slam your dunk.
You know you're being most unfair.
All I did was throw a chair.

Now you've really lost your cool;
acting like an utter fool.
Demanding I sit down, that's fine,
my chair's out on the free throw line!

Yet you say, "Get off the court,
or to the locker room report!"
See, ref, you aren't worth a dime.
Guess I'll just bring two chairs next time.

Then one day I got to see
just what it was to referee.
For then I donned the striped shirt
and found out just how much it hurt.

When all the people called ME blind,
and one lone friend I could not find.
They said my lack of intelligence
had ruined the game for these 10 gents.

Well after that my feelings changed;
my attitude I rearranged.
The referee is just a man
and he just does the best he can.

No one could all the fouls detect,
so referee, you've my respect.
I really plan to be more kind,
because good refs are hard to find.

But referee, you must remember,
from that first jump ball in November
Up until the season's end,
that you're no god among mere men.

For you have got to realize
that it will be to your demise
If you infer to one and all
that you just NEVER miss a call.

'Cause when you have that attitude
players scream and fans throw food
Coaches snarl, stomp, and fight,
'cause no mere man is always right.

So don't let that head of yours swell
when you think you've done so well.
Be humble as you make each call,
'cause only God could call them all.

APPLICATION SUGGESTIONS:

1. Respect all referees throughout the game, knowing that they are doing their best but, like you, they sometimes make mistakes.

2. Compliment referees during the game (for a correct call, even one that didn't go your way).

3. Help the referees in any way you can (retrieving a loose ball, etc).

4. Let a Christ-like attitude be consistently displayed in all situations, and the referee (who is human and impressionable just like everyone else) will be affected in a positive way by your behavior. *"Live your life in such a way that someone who doesn't know God but knows you will come to know God because he knows you."*

18

RESPONSE

"All who listen to my instructions and follow them are wise, like a man who builds his house on solid rock....But those who hear my instructions and ignore them are foolish, like a man who builds his house on sand" (Matthew 7:24, 26, TLB).

"Anyone who loves learning accepts criticism, but a person who hates being corrected is stupid" (Proverbs 12:1, TLB).

Much of our success in life is dependent upon our response to instruction and correction we receive from parents, teachers, employers, coaches, and God. Many responses are in vogue today: blaming someone else, making excuses, questioning validity, questioning authority, whining, ignoring. Although popular, all of these responses will inevitably have negative consequences, not only for the individual but also for the organization that individual represents.

The children of Israel wandered in the desert for 40 years because of their inadequate response to God's instruction. They whined, blamed God, questioned His authority and wisdom, and ignored His instructions. It is the ultimate illustration of improper response and the consequences of disobedience. Their lack of faith, even after all the miracles God had performed on their behalf, seems incredible to us. But before we become too self-righteous in our condemnation of these amazingly stubborn people, let us check out our own response to God's instructions. When God's instructions don't match your wants and desires, how do you respond? Do you really trust God? Are you willing to accept a "no" or "wait" answer to prayer? When you pray for God's will, are you willing to accept His will even though it may differ from yours? Your response to instruction and correction from God will ultimately be a test of faith. Do you really believe God knows best? If so, your response will be a simple "Yes, Lord." Your trust and obedience will bring an awesome peace to your life.

A player's response to his coach's instruction and correction is critical to the team's success. Improper responses would include the following:

1. *Excuses.* Don't focus on clearing yourself when you are being corrected by explaining away your actions. "I'm tired." "My shoes hurt my feet." "The referee got in the way." "Sweat got in my eyes." Don't waste the coach's time with such excuses. When you are in a defensive mode it's very difficult to make good use of correction.

2. *Blame.* It's always someone else's fault -- your teammates, the referees, the coach, Mom & Dad. John Wooden said, *"A man may make mistakes, but he isn't a failure until he starts blaming someone else."*

3. *Whining.* Get out of the self-pity mode, accept the fact that you need this instruction and correction, and listen to your coach.

4. *Ignore.* When you do not pay attention to, or follow, your coach's instructions or listen to his corrections for you, such actions will have major negative consequences. Not only does the coach probably know more than you about the issue

76

at hand, but it is also his job as coach to instruct and correct. As a player, it's your role to listen, trust, and obey. When you defy the coach you are setting your team up for major problems.

5. *Diversion.* "But what about him?" This is a great tactic for circumventing any correction that may come your way. Humbled by Jesus' three consecutive "Do you love me" questions, Peter used this diversion tactic rather than deal with Jesus' instruction and correction. Instead of responding to this admonition and his own shortcomings, Peter responded, "What about him, Lord?" pointing to the disciple John. Jesus replied, "If I want him to live until I return, what is that to you? You follow me" (John 21:22, TLB). In other words, we're not worrying about someone else right now, we're just trying to straighten *you* out.

The above are all examples of the wrong response to correction and instruction. As Christians, our one correct response is, "Yes, Lord," spoken in a genuine attitude of trust as we joyfully acknowledge that God knows what is best for us. And, even though we realize that coaches are not perfect like God, they are in positions of authority and leadership which would dictate to us that our response, as players, should simply be "Yes, Coach, I'll do my best." Such a response by a player is absolutely essential if you are serious about improving and if your team will be able to approach its maximum level of efficiency.

"Blame is the coward's way out."
        --Elvin Hayes

"One thing I don't believe in: excuses."
        --Karl Malone

77

APPLICATION SUGGESTIONS:

1. Although you may disagree with your coach on occasions, it is rarely appropriate to take issue with what he says in front of a group. Most of the time it is best to express your concerns and opinions in a one on one setting with the coach.

2. Although it is human nature to us to be defensive when we are criticized or corrected, make a commitment to be receptive when you are corrected by your coach.

3. Understand that criticism/correction from your coach is intended for you and the entire team to get better. Coaches who do not point out mistakes and offer solutions are not good coaches. How can you get better if you don't know what you did wrong or how you can correct it?

19

ROLES

"The body is a unit, though it is made up of many parts; and though all of its parts are many, they form one body ... The eye cannot say to the hand, 'I don't need you!' On the contrary, those parts of the body that seem to be weaker are indispensable..." (1 Corinthians 12:21-22, NIV).

Do you realize that God has a very special role for you and me to play in building His Kingdom? Too often, however, instead of enthusiastically accepting our role, we tend to either long for another "more important" role or resist our role because of feelings of inadequacy or fear. God had a difficult time convincing Moses that he could fulfill the role He had planned for him. Instead of welcoming such an important role Moses was amazingly reluctant. His feelings of inadequacy (and lack of faith) caused him to plead with God to release him from this lofty calling. Conversely, the desire to be recognized and exalted by men causes countless Christians to seek roles which would result in fame and fortune, resisting God's actual plan for their lives.

Either way, when we do not embrace the unique role God has mapped out just for us we ultimately fail to fulfill our Christian calling to spread the Gospel and be a servant of Christ. As we seek to identify our role in God's great plan through prayer and a receptive spirit, God will reveal to us what we are to do. And when He does, we must joyfully accept our role and trust God to help us fulfill our calling. We also need to remember that *all* roles are important. We can't all be Billy Graham or Mother Teresa, but God will honor our efforts to live out His plan for us, no matter how insignificant it may seem.

Brother Lawrence is a shining example of accepting God's plan for him with humility and enthusiasm. He took great pride and honor in such menial tasks as caring for the kitchen in the monastery. He did not spend his time yearning for another more visible task, one that would be noticed by many and that would better feed his ego. Brother Lawrence simply concentrated on accessing God as, day after day, he joyfully went about doing his best to fulfill God's calling for his life in virtual anonymity. He found true contentment within the will and presence of God. As God's obedient servant he never preached a single sermon, yet his thoughts and his life were recorded and he is now an inspiration to millions of Christians.

Understanding, accepting, and giving 100% effort to fulfilling your particular role on the basketball team is critical to the efficiency of your unit. This is not an easy task. Scottie Pippen, a key member of the Michael Jordan-led Chicago Bulls' championship team remarked, "Sometimes a player's greatest challenge is coming to grips with his role on the team." Although we would all like to be the leading scorer—the one who gets the headlines—we must realize the impossibility of everyone having this dream fulfilled. If we are focused on team goals, however, we are not as concerned with personal glory as with contributing to the efficiency of the team, and we're more than likely to accept a less glamorous role.

If you're not sure of your role on the team, talk to the coach. He will define it for you. If your attitude is, "What can I do to best help this team win?" you will accept your role and pursue it with gusto. Just as Brother Lawrence was determined to be the best kitchen man he could be, so you should pursue your role on the team with equal enthusiasm and desire. If your assignment is to set good picks to allow your leading scorer to get open, become the best, most efficient screener the game of basketball has ever known. If your job is to get the ball safely up the court and initiate the offense, be determined to become the best ball-handler and passer in the building. Neither of the above roles will result in much publicity or acclaim. But your coach and your teammates know that such anonymous, non-statistical skills as setting good screens and getting the ball up the court safely are essential to the team's success.

So remember to identify, accept, and enthusiastically pursue your role, whether as a Christian or a basketball player. It is vitally important to the success of yourself and your team. How comforting and encouraging to realize that all roles, no matter how small or insignificant they may appear, are important. And the successful fulfillment of *all* roles will lead to great satisfaction and reward.

APPLICATION SUGGESTIONS:

1. Meet with your coach with the purpose of clearly defining your role on the team. What does the coach expect of you?
2. Commit to fulfilling your role thoroughly and completely with gusto. Embracing your role enables you to grow as a person and helps your team get better.

81

3. Understand that whatever our life is all about, we are to represent Christ in our attitudes and actions at all times, because God will use us all to further His kingdom.

"There are people with a lot more talent than I have who have been weeded out of the league because they couldn't put their egos aside to fill a role."
--Curt Rambis

20

SELF-SUFFICIENCY

"Seek ye first the Kingdom of God, and his righteousness; and all these things shall be added unto you" (Matthew 6:33, KJ).

My friend seemed to have everything going in the right direction. He was a kindhearted individual who had a good job, a loving wife, and two small children. But at age 25 this active, athletic individual found himself in a hospital. He had so much pain in his back that even heavy doses of painkillers could not alleviate his constant suffering. The cause of this sudden onslaught of pain was unknown and the doctors could not even pinpoint what exactly was wrong. Then, to compound the frustration, his infant son became violently ill and was admitted to the same hospital. So intense was his pain, however, that my friend could not even get out of bed to see his son, who was just two floors down.

The feeling of helplessness was overwhelming, but at that moment my friend fully realized that there were things in life that he couldn't control. As successful and self-sufficient as he had become, at this moment he was able to acknowledge his need of God. Self-sufficiency will only take you so far. In the end, we all need God. My friend and his son both fully recovered, and the experience made him even more Christ-like and humble.

In your prosperity and successes have you, consciously or unconsciously, decided that you have such a firm handle on your life that you really don't need God anymore? Self-sufficiency—being in total control of your life—is a great feeling, but it eventually will catch up to you, just as it did my friend. We're never quite as self-sufficient as we think we are. If we leave God out of the picture and start handling life on our own, Satan will eventually overwhelm and defeat us. We are no match for Satan. We need God. Jesus tells us that the most important thing we can do is love God, not ourselves. Only by trusting God and submitting your will to His can you triumph over Satan and achieve the ultimate victory.

In the same way, you cannot take a self-important, self-sufficient, "I don't need anyone else" attitude onto the court and expect to win a basketball game. If you have a real need to be in total control, take up a sport like golf or tennis, but stay away from basketball. As talented as you may be, you cannot single-handedly win game after game. In a team sport like basketball, self-sufficiency is more likely to tear a team apart rather than win games. Do you realize that the winner of the scoring title in the NBA is rarely a member of the championship team?

One of the beautiful aspects of basketball is that one person cannot win the game all by himself. He needs help. Just as the Christian needs God to win in the game of life, the basketball player needs his teammates in order to be victorious on the court. Kareem Abdul Jabbar, who scored more points than any player in the history of the NBA, once said, "We play as a team. One-man teams are losing teams." So even the most prolific scorer basketball has ever known acknowledges the dangers of the self-sufficient, "I don't need anybody else" attitude.

As Christians we must acknowledge the fact that we can't make it without God, just as a basketball player must realize that victory cannot be achieved without the help of his teammates. Don't accept this reality grudgingly but with an attitude of joy and anticipation. When we embrace our teammates, just as when we embrace God, we immediately become stronger—a more potent force. That's exciting! We accomplish so much more when we shove aside our own self-sufficiency in order to receive the help God and our teammates can give us. Then we're really on the road to ultimate triumph and to becoming the best that we can be.

"Generally speaking, individuals don't win basketball games."
-- John Wooden

"We really do need each other."
--Reuben Welch

"God is our strength and refuge, an ever present help in trouble" (Psalm 46:1, NIV).

APPLICATION SUGGESTIONS:

1. Do you only acknowledge God when things are going poorly for you? If so, work hard on your attitude. Give Him credit in all good things as well, in this way avoiding the dangerous self-sufficiency attitude that can so easily creep in and infect.
2. Work hard to give others credit rather than beating your own drum. When you make a basket, acknowledge the teammate that threw the good pass or set the good screen to get you open, rather than beating your chest and yelling in a display of "Look how good I am."

21

TEAMWORK

"The greatest players fit with the team. They play within the team's style rather than asking the team to change its style."
  --Jack Ramsay

"Some people believe you win with your five best players, but I found that you win with the five who fit together best."
  --Red Auerbach

"All the believers were together and had everything in common ... Every day they continued to meet together in the temple courts. They broke bread in their homes and ate together with glad and sincere hearts, praising God and enjoying the favor of all the people" (Acts 2:44, 46-7, TLB).

One of the greatest definitions of teamwork can be found when we look at the early Church. The new Christians from the Apostle Paul's era were not only in the minority, but also were not at all popular with the majority. Yet as difficult as the world at that time made it on them, they still managed to not only survive, but also multiply. And when the mighty Roman Empire finally collapsed, the people they persecuted—the Christians--continued to thrive.

How could this happen? The Romans used a considerable amount of teamwork to forge the greatest empire history has ever known. Unfortunately, greed, selfishness, moral decay, and lust for power began to dominate the ruling Roman organization until its collapse was eminent. Conversely, the early Christians were able to withstand the persecution they encountered because of the teamwork in their organization.

Both the Roman Empire and the early Christians had teams, but it takes more than just having people on a team to make that team efficient. True teamwork in any organization requires its participants to put the welfare of the team ahead of their own personal agenda. This is why the early Christians survived. They helped and supported their Christian brothers and sisters in any way they could, each giving sacrificially and joyfully to others in need.

As a Christian, do you focus on helping your Christian peers? Or are you too involved with your own wants and needs to be a true servant? It is true that we have the ultimate teammate in Jesus to help us on our journey, but God fully intended the team to be much larger than two. We must tune in to the needs of fellow believers, both physical and spiritual. Being a Christian in today's society is extremely difficult, just as it was for the early Christians. We need to be true team players by praying for others on a consistent basis and by our regular attendance and participation at church functions. We do this primarily for the nurture and support of our fellow Christians, not necessarily for our own benefit. *"And pray in the spirit on all occasions with all kinds of prayers and requests. With this in mind, be alert and always keep on praying for all the saints"* (Ephesians 6:18, NIV).

A fully efficient basketball team must display the same type of teamwork. The true team player offers support, encouragement, and help to his teammates. Your teammates' needs must take priority over your own needs and goals in order for the team to function at maximum efficiency. Rather than focusing on how many points you score or how many minutes you play, focus instead on how you can help your teammates and your team be better.

Nowhere in basketball is teamwork more in evidence than on defense. While it is true that good screens, ball movement, and timely passes are important, offenses often feature the best scorer going one-on-one while everybody else stays out of the way. Defense, however, requires all five players to work as a helping, reacting, communicating, rotating unit, because invariably your opponent has at least a couple of scorers who are very difficult for just one player to stop. Good defenses, working as a unit, can effectively stop an individual who is virtually unstoppable in a one-on-one situation.

That's teamwork. And that's what it takes to reach your full potential as a basketball team. Bill Walton said, *"Winning is about having the whole team on the same page."* This has to start with the proper attitude. The true team player takes an "all-for-one-and-one-for-all" approach, placing team goals above individual goals. Only then can teamwork take place. It's a beautiful thing to see and experience.

"In basketball personal goals have little meaning. Team goals are the only ones that really matter."
--Jack Ramsay

"It's amazing how much can be accomplished if no one cares who gets the credit."
--John Wooden

APPLICATION SUGGESTIONS:

1. Be a constant encourager for your teammates, whether they do well or mess up. Leave the criticism to the coach.
2. Understand that when a player knows his teammates have his back he usually plays much better because he is not dealing with anxiety or fear of failure.
3. Remember, nobody wants to let their teammates down. So when they mess up they do not need your wrath or disapproval, they need your support.

22

THE ENEMY

"Woe unto you, teachers of the law and Pharisees, you hypocrites" (Matthew 23: 13, 15, 23, 27, 29, NIV)!

"Get behind me, Satan!" - Jesus' words to Peter, recorded in Mark 8:33, TLB.

The history of Christianity has been fraught with a variety of forces that would steer an individual *away* from the Lord.   From the outset, governmental persecution (by the Romans) was a major problem and this is still frighteningly evident in many countries in the world today.   Although Christians living in America are now seeing a subtle, yet consistent, attempt by certain entities to rid this great nation of God altogether, we still enjoy the freedom to worship our Lord without undue harassment.

But there remain other potent threats to Christ-like living.   There is a moral decay of society. Addictions like gambling, alcohol, and other drugs are destructive forces. There is a heightened prevalence of adultery, divorce, and the break-up of the family. Material gain has become a no-holds-barred, all-consuming quest. There is a growing indifference to and acceptance of sin.

With all these tools at his disposal, Satan has been successful in separating man from God. But his *greatest* tool can be found in congregations across the nation every Sunday. Some Christians claim to be holy but live in sin. They are pious on Sunday but promiscuous on Monday, talking the talk but not walking the walk. They turn more people away from God than all the other factors listed above. Isn't it interesting that Jesus saved his greatest wrath and condemnation for the religious community? As Christians, we need to understand and deal with the many factors which can lure us away from God. We also need to realize that the *greatest* enemy of Christianity is a segment of the Christian community itself ... hypocritical believers.

So what can we do about it? How can we avoid being our own worst enemy? First of all, we must not come across as pious, judgmental, or "holier than thou." Secondly, we must not discount or accept sin. It is a very popular notion in current society to downplay the existence of any absolute truths. We often hear, "everything is relative," or "whatever works for you." But sin is still sin. The Scriptures have not changed. Homosexuality, adultery, and cheating are still sins, no matter how much society now accepts them. Truth is still truth. Thirdly, just as important as hating sin is our love and compassion for the sinner. While condemning her sin Jesus showed compassion to the sinner when he rescued the women caught in adultery. As Christians we need to be genuine and authentic. Be part of the solution, not part of the problem.

Sometimes our success on the basketball court is hindered by our failure to look *within* to identify the problem. Too often we cite our circumstances or the actions of others as the source of our problems. We blame incompetent referees, hostile crowds, poor coaching decisions, or a long bus trip. But just as the deadliest enemy to Christianity can be the Christian, so the major reason for inefficiency on the basketball court can be found when we look inward. The basketball player, like the Christian, must have the correct approach to ensure success. When you dwell on the fact that you've never beaten this team in their gym before, or the fact that they have a good record, or the fact that they beat you earlier this season, you are virtually guaranteeing a loss. So when things aren't going as well as they should, whether on the court or in life, look within yourself *first* to identify and solve the problem. Remember, more often than not, the enemy is *us.*

"Don't criticize, and then you won't be criticized. For others will treat you the way you treat them. And why worry about a speck in the eye of your brother when you already have a board in your own eye? Should you say, 'Friend, let me help you get the speck out of your eye' when you can't even see because of the board in your own?' Hypocrite! First get rid of the board. Then you can see to help your brother" (Matthew 7:1-5, TLB).

APPLICATION SUGGESTIONS:

1. In a society that is drifting steadily away from God and His Word, are you part of the problem or part of the solution?
2. List some of the specific ways you can be part of the solution in today's society.
3. Understand that the enemy (Satan) is smarter and more devious than you. Therefore pray continually for guidance and direction. The Holy Spirit will help you resist Satan's schemes. *"Submit yourselves, then, to God. Resist the devil and he will flee from you"* (James 4:7, NIV).

23

TOMORROW

"So don't be anxious about tomorrow. God will take care of your tomorrows too. Live one day at a time" (Matthew 6:34, TLB).

How often do you think about the future? Whether it's what you want to be doing twenty years from now or what you plan to do later in the day, we all seem to spend a lot of our time thinking about the future. And there's really nothing wrong with planning and thinking ahead. Often it's very wise and prudent to do so, but we've got to realize that every second we spend with our thoughts on the future negates the present. How many times, for example, have you not really heard a word someone was saying to you because you were busy thinking about what you were going to say when it was your turn?

The great thing about being a Christian is that our tomorrows have already been taken care of. God has promised to take care of all of our needs if we simply surrender our will to His and trust Him. How many opportunities for service do we waste or not even recognize because we're too consumed with concern and anticipation for our future? How many people promise God that they will start tithing as soon as some bills get paid off, or that they will start going to church as soon as the kids get older? Don't get caught up in this trap. If we are sincere about fulfilling our mission as Christians we must focus on the present, alert and anticipating opportunities God will give to us to spread the Gospel to a needy world. Tomorrow is the future; it's later. Don't let today pass you by without giving it the attention it deserves.

Basketball history is filled with stories of teams who, as they anticipated the big showdown game with their arch-rival on Saturday, overlooked a lesser opponent in the mid-week game and ended up losing a game they figured to win easily. Had they given their full focus on that game (the present) rather than on the game on the weekend (the future), the result would most likely have been different. In late February 2014, Syracuse was the undefeated, #1 ranked NCAA Division I basketball team, having won 21 consecutive games. One of those wins was an epic overtime win over Duke, a much publicized match-up against two legendary coaches: Syracuse's Coach Boeheim and Duke's Coach K. The much-anticipated rematch at Duke was scheduled for the next Saturday. Duke was ranked #5 in the nation. So how did the midweek games go? Duke lost to unranked North Carolina and Syracuse lost at home to Boston College, who was 2-10 in conference play. Could it be that even two of the most accomplished, knowledgeable coaches in NCAA history could not prevent their players from looking ahead to the Saturday showdown? Whether looking ahead was a factor in these unexpected losses is not known for sure, but the fact that the future can often affect, either consciously or unconsciously, our focus or intensity on the present is a reality that we must deal with.

The best players and the best teams, although they have goals which can only be realized in the future, spend their time totally focused on today. If it's the Thursday practice before the big game, they are totally focused and intense throughout practice. If it's pre-season practice and games are still a month away, they are going 100% on all the fundamental drills and suicides so that they can be best prepared when the season begins. If it is July they are going to practice good habits in pick-up games, refusing to play lazy, not hustle, or foul frequently. They value the present. They're making the most of today's opportunities.

So take full advantage of today and the opportunities it holds by giving the present your undivided attention. Full focus on today will make you a better player tomorrow. Do you want to be a winner? Do you want to be the best you can be? Bobby Knight claims that the will to win is overrated, simply because *everyone* wants to win. But it is the will to *prepare* to win that makes the difference. Basketball players don't wait until game day to prepare to win. They prepare to win in practice, whether it is in the off-season, pre-season, or the day before the game.

Do you apply game intensity to practice? If not, you're hurting yourself and your team. Value today, and then your tomorrows will be much more pleasant and rewarding.

Practice doesn't make perfect; perfect practice makes perfect.
    --Vince Lombardi

"Failing to prepare is preparing to fail."
    --John Wooden

APPLICATION SUGGESTIONS:

1. Instead of focusing so much on when Jesus is coming again, if there will be a pre-tribulation rapture, or who is the Anti-Christ, and other such futuristic topics, why not spend all your time and energy on what you can do TODAY to further God's Kingdom?

2. Understand that it will be no problem to get up for a big game; so focus on reaching the same degree of up for preseason and offseason workouts.

3. If your focus is on today, be confident that God will provide opportunities for you to, in some way, help further His Kingdom. Expect them. *"Yesterday is history; tomorrow is a mystery; today is a gift, that's why it's called the present."*

4. *"Make each day a masterpiece." - John Wooden*

24

WINNING

"The important thing in the Olympic Games is not winning but taking part. The essential thing in life is not conquering but fighting well."

--Pierre de Coubertin, founder of the modern Olympic Games.

"You can win and still not succeed, still not achieve what you should. And you can lose without really failing at all."
--Bobby Knight

Everybody wants to be a winner. People tend to admire winners—they are looked up to and sometimes become heroes to many. They gain the exalted positions in society and often become role models. At the time Jesus was preaching and teaching on earth, the acknowledged winners of the religious world were the Pharisees. They had scored more points than anyone else by their extensive knowledge of the law and their meticulous adherence to the countless laws that were, at that time, the measure of a man's religious worth. Pharisees held the exalted status among the Jews. They were looked up to and were considered winners.

Or were they? Jesus certainly didn't think so. His greatest wrath was poured out onto these "winners" as He exposed and condemned their hypocrisy. Although they were winners in the eyes of the world, Jesus clearly and adamantly labeled them losers. Their accomplishments had resulted in a winner's label, but their attitudes--merciless and self-righteous— earned them the severest condemnation from the Son of God.

In his Sermon on the Mount Jesus indicates that if our attitudes are not better than that of the Pharisees we will never even make it to heaven (Matthew 5:20). So it sounds like the Pharisees may have won the battle but lost the war. They achieved a winner label on earth in the eyes of men, but they were labeled as hypocrites and losers by Jesus and are spending eternity in hell. So maybe winning isn't all it's cracked up to be. Or maybe we're just using the wrong definition. Maybe the winner isn't necessarily just the team that scores the most points, the one who crosses the finish line first, or the one who makes the most money. You tend to acquire the winner's label and exalted status when you ace an exam. The acclaim of your peers, parents, teachers, and your own ego are very satisfying, but if you cheated on the exam your label from Jesus will be the same as He gave the Pharisees. It comes down to who you are really trying to please or impress—the world or your Savior. Consider the consequences as you make this decision.

So should a basketball team quit trying to win? Of course not. The objective of the game is to do everything you can, *within the rules*, to score the most points. The key is to not sacrifice your character or integrity in pursuit of the victory. Don't allow yourself to get caught up in the "win-at-all-costs" philosophy which unfortunately pervades athletics in current society. Don't allow yourself to place all the value of your participation on the final score. The most successful coaches in the history of basketball have defined winning and success in a fashion that does not include the final score as the bottom line. UCLA's legendary coach John Wooden said, "Doing the best you are capable of doing is victory in itself, and less than that is defeat." Coach Mike Krzyzewski of Duke commented, "Our goal is not to win. It's to play together and play hard. Then, winning takes care of itself."

The final score never justifies holding someone's jersey, elbowing, grabbing, or in any way sacrificing your integrity and character on the court. Don't be proud of not getting caught. Be proud of maintaining your character, integrity, and intensity throughout the game, regardless of the circumstances. Value the journey. Give it your absolute best shot from start to finish, no matter what the situation. Then you will truly be a winner, no matter what the final score of the game. True winners are in heaven. Pharisees aren't.

"Success is never final. Failure is never fatal. It's courage that counts."
    --John Wooden

APPLICATION SUGGESTIONS:

1. Write a paragraph that defines winning, expressing what it is and what it isn't.
2. What is most important to you when playing a game?
3. Give some specific examples of what "winning at all costs" might mean in a basketball game.
4. How would you describe a Christian who is a winner?

25

YESTERDAY

I'm free from the guilt that I carried,
*   From the dull empty life I'm set free;*
For when I met Jesus He made me complete;
*   He forgot the foolish man I used to be.*

I'm free from the fear of tomorrow;
*   I'm free from the guilt of the past;*
I've traded my shackles for a glorious song;
*   I'm free, praise the Lord, free at last.*
*   --Bill & Gloria Gaither*

Freedom is a marvelous thing to possess. When we are truly free we do not have anything standing in our way as we tackle the various situations we encounter in life. What a great advantage! Only when we are truly free can we maximize our efficiency in the tasks we undertake, totally unencumbered and able to apply full focus to our efforts.

God, in His amazing grace, has promised to forgive our sins, *all* of them, if we repent of our sins and surrender our will to His. This allows us the freedom, as new creatures in Christ, to focus on living our lives in a Christ-like manner.

But how often we undermine the freedom God gives us by failing to forgive *ourselves* of past sins and indiscretions! Guilt is one of the most effective weapons of Satan. We can never be free to live our life as Christ wants us to if we cannot fully accept God's forgiveness and let go of yesterday's sins and the accompanying guilt. Guilt undermines our freedom, ruins our focus, destroys our confidence, and attacks our self-worth. It really comes down to a matter of faith. God is indeed able to free us from the guilt of our past as long as we trust Him fully. We can only defeat Satan and the guilt he plagues us with if we call on the name of Jesus. Until we come to this point we cannot live the life of a Christian—spreading the Good News and helping others see Christ through us—because we're too consumed and discouraged by our own struggles.

Basketball players have a similar problem with the past. Your ability as a player to deal with all aspects of the past in basketball will greatly influence your effectiveness on the court. From what happened when you played this team last year to what just happened two seconds ago in the current game, the past can have a great impact on the present in a basketball contest. If you're playing on the road against a team you have never beaten you would be wise to erase that fact, and all the connotations that go with it, from your memory as you mentally prepare for the upcoming game. A popular song in the 1960's had this phrase, "...but that was yesterday, and yesterday's gone." That is exactly the approach you need to take in the above scenario. Keep the past out of the present, keep fear out of the picture, and keep your confidence high for the moment.

In a game, players may let the immediate past affect their effectiveness. How many times have you seen a player make a bad pass and then allow the resulting guilt, remorse, or anger lead to more mistakes? Sometimes they commit an unwise foul in an overzealous attempt to make up for the bad pass or assign blame to a teammate or official. He or she might stop, shoulders slumped, in a brief episode of self-pity and self-doubt while his or her man scores a lay-up at the other end? In any case, your failure to accept your failure and move on ruins your focus and hurts your own performance as well as that of your team. So don't allow your present to be compromised because you can't stop thinking about the past. All players make mistakes, but in basketball you often don't have time to dwell on them. Focus on the present. Forget the past. Don't let the emotional results of what you *did* affect what you *do*. In both basketball and Christianity, we cannot allow the guilt of the past to rob us from the freedom of the present, and our ability to be the absolute best we can possibly be.

It should be noted, however, that before the past is totally forgotten we must, at some point, learn from it. Our successes and failures from the past should be analyzed and processed so that we may be more effective in the present and future when similar scenarios recur. Good coaches use the half-time break to process the good and the bad of the first half and instruct their team on the adjustments and procedures that need to be made in order to be more efficient in the second half. Players should go through the same process regarding their own individual performances. So we should be wise in recognizing the past as a valuable teacher, but we should also be wise enough to refrain from *dwelling* on the past.

"As far as the east is from the west, so far has He removed our transgressions from us" (Psalm 103:12, NIV).

"No, dear brothers, I am still not all I should be, but I am bringing all my energy to bear on this one thing; forgetting the past and looking forward to what lies ahead, I strain to reach the end of the race and receive the prize for which God is

calling us up to heaven, because of what Christ Jesus did for us" (Philippians 3:13-14, TLB).

APPLICATION SUGGESTIONS:

1. Identify the past situations in your life that you cannot forget and that keep you from being your best in the present. Remember, the Holy Spirit will help you deal with your past.
2. Are you holding any grudges? If so, they will continue to hinder your present. Therefore, deal with the source of the grudge with honesty and compassion, and then you should be free to move on.
3. Remember, nothing is more freeing than forgiveness, both to the one who forgives and to the one who is forgiven.

Made in the USA
Monee, IL
07 November 2024

69585402R00059